AUDIT COMMISSIONS:
REVIEWING THE
REVIEWERS

audit
commissions

reviewing the reviewers

Kate Jones + Scott Prasser

connorcourt
PUBLISHING

Published in 2013 by Connor Court Publishing Pty Ltd

Copyright © Kate Jones and Scott Prasser 2013

PO Box 224W
Ballarat VIC 3350
sales@connorcourt.com
www.connorcourt.com

ISBN: 9781922168993 (pbk.)

Cover design by Ian James

Printed in Australia

CONTENTS

Government, Policy and Politics Series

A partnership between Connor Court Publishing and Public Policy Institute, Australian Catholic University

Audit Commissions: Reviewing the Reviewers by Kate Jones and Scott Prasser is part of the **Government, Policy and Politics Series**, a joint initiative of Connor Court Publishing and the Public Policy Institute (PPI), Australian Catholic University (ACU). The series seeks to explore past, present and future developments in Australian government, policy and politics.

The Public Policy Institute is a public policy think tank undertaking policy relevant research, analysis and commentary on important issues on the public agenda and actively engages with the wider policy community.

Kate Jones is Research Fellow at ACU's Public Policy Institute, with qualifications in politics, economics and librarianship. After researching and writing about parliaments, parliamentary committees and parliamentarians, Kate has focussed in her recent research on aspects of public and social policy. She has also worked for state and federal governments and in two parliaments.

Scott Prasser was the inaugural Executive Director of the Public Policy Institute at ACU and previously worked in senior policy and research positions in federal and state governments. He has written extensively on Australian public policy and politics and in 2006 published, *Royal Commissions and Public Inquiries in Australia*.

Series Editor: Professor Scott Prasser, Executive Director, Public Policy Institute, Australian Catholic University.

Books in the Series:

Gary Johns, *Right Social Justice – Better Ways to Help the Poor* (2012)

Graeme Starr, *Carrick: Principles, Policy and Politics* (2012)

Ian Hancock, *Greiner: A Political Biography* (2013)

John Nethercote, Scott Prasser & Nicholas Aroney, (eds), *Her Majesty's Loyal Oppositions* (2013)

Scott Prasser & Helen Tracey, *Royal Commissions and Public Inquiries – Practice and Potential* (2014)

1

The importance of commissions of audit

Introduction

In 1988, the newly elected government of New South Wales appointed a body to examine the finances of the state. It was called the *New South Wales Commission of Audit*. This was the first of 14 such bodies established under various names by Australian Commonwealth, state and territory governments over the next 25 years. Their role, as described by the governments that appointed them, was to examine the economic and financial situation and make recommendations about how to improve it. With one exception they were appointed by incoming Liberal Party governments, National-Liberal or Liberal-National Party coalitions and in most cases those governments had defeated long-term incumbent Labor governments at a time of economic and financial stress.

The new governments usually sought to blame their predecessors for these economic and financial problems, and promoted the commissions of audit as independent expert bodies that would review the state of finances and public administration, and propose solutions to the perceived financial problems and malaise in the administrations they had inherited. The solutions that the commissions proposed invariably included: restructuring of government departments; outsourcing of services; privatisation or corporatisation of government bodies; and cuts in government spending and public sector employment. In some cases they also involved a fundamental rethinking of what government is and does. Their agenda coincided with growing acceptance of what has been variously described as that of 'New Public Management' (NPM) (Aucoin 1995; Hood 1990; 1991; 1995; Zifcak 1994), neoliberalism, or, in Australia, economic rationalism (Pusey 1991), with its emphasis on applying private sector techniques, market principles, balanced budgets, and reducing the size and reach of government. It was also the era of what Power (1997) has designated as the audit explosion – of increasing attempts to measure, monitor, and review the performance of government agencies, programs, and policies. A concept that was once part of the practice of accounting spread beyond its original definition to "environmental audit, value for money audit, management audit, forensic audit, data audit, intellectual property audit, medical audit, teaching audit, and technology audit" (Power 1997: 3).

Why study commissions of audit?

Though audit commissions shared several traits with public inquiries – being temporary, ad hoc bodies appointed by executive government with members drawn mostly from outside government, and with some processes of public consultation and reporting (Banks 2013) – they nevertheless represented a new or different institution in Australian government, and deserve our attention for several reasons.

First and foremost, audit commissions were generally perceived to have a more overt ideological bent than usual public inquiries, where the emphasis has been on both providing, and appearing to provide, independent, non-partisan, expert advice.

Second, audit commissions had, by their very appointment by the incoming government and their terms of reference to review the previous administration's finances, a closer connection to government compared to public inquiries that aim to be seen as being at arm's length from the government that has appointed them.

Third, in seeking to provide an accurate picture of the state of finances, they sometimes temporarily supplanted – if not wholly replaced and challenged – existing permanent budgetary bodies such as treasury and finance departments in ways that had not occurred previously. However, in some instances, finance departments also saw audit commissions as vehicles to achieve the expenditure cuts they had been unable to impose.

Fourth, they had a more expansive whole-of-government brief in pinpointing areas of poor administration, program delivery, and misallocation of funds, than traditional review agencies, such as auditors-general or specific public inquiries.

Fifth, their emphasis on priority setting and the need for greater whole-of-government coordination was more structured and ruthlessly stated than that of other central agencies, such as departments of the premier and cabinet, or the prime minister and cabinet.

Sixth, given how most governments appointed audit commissions as one of their first acts – and placed great store in their role of tackling the initial financial 'crises,' and in providing future directions for the government – audit commissions have initially appeared to wield more influence, albeit sometimes briefly, than the other more usual public inquiries that are often criticised for their apparent impotence. Audit commissions also, for a time, seem more influential than other political arms of modern government, such as ministerial staff, party headquarters, ministers and backbenchers.

Seventh, despite their proliferation since 1988, audit commissions, as a distinct institution, have received only a limited mention in the academic literature. General accounts of public sector reform and finance in Australia (Davis and Rhodes 2000; O'Faircheallaigh, Wanna and Weller 1999), and recent macro-surveys of Australian politics and institutions (Galligan and Roberts 2007), have ignored them.

Detailed accounts of audit commissions have been limited to one-off single jurisdictional reviews concerning particular commissions (Hayward 1999, Victoria; Wanna, Kelly and Forster 2000: 246-248, Commonwealth) or studies of a particular aspect of their recommendations (Ryan 1998). Even some of the key protagonists that appointed them make only passing reference to their appointment (Costello 2008: 96), or no reference at all (Howard: 2011). Where commissions have been considered as distinct instruments of review, the analysis is now dated (Walsh 1995).

Eighth, although audit commissions in Australia have been appointed almost exclusively by the non-Labor side of politics, their repeated use (despite a hiatus from 1996 to 2008 – see Table 1) over three decades, and the fact that the new incoming Abbott Coalition Commonwealth Government (2013) has appointed a new audit commission, means they have become part of Australian government architecture.

Ninth, audit commissions are essentially a new instrument of government that do not fit easily with existing institutional arrangements and processes. Although there are precedents for similar types of bodies being appointed in the past, at both Commonwealth and state levels, such bodies did not conform to the same basic type, structure and nomenclature (see below).

Last, audit commissions as they are structured and operated are very much an Australian phenomenon. There are few comparative overseas equivalents. In the United States, the 1984 Grace Commission on Waste (*Private Sector Survey on Cost Control*) that reported to the Reagan Government was a one-off initiative with certain similar features. However, in the United Kingdom, the Conservative Thatcher Administration pursued cutbacks and many of the same elements of NPM as in Australia – eschewing external public bodies, such as audit commissions, and using internal mechanisms, such as the Efficiency Unit embedded in the Prime Minister's office in Downing Street. Of course, there was in the United Kingdom the Audit Commission for Local Government, but it was established in 1983 as an ongoing body to overview local government finances, and, later, the National Health Service; it has since been disbanded. It was very different to the whole-of-government, ad hoc, audit commissions established in Australia.

Issues about commissions of audit

This book seeks to identify and analyse the reasons for appointing commissions of audit, to identify their roles, processes, basic thrusts and impact, and to assess their place in Australian government. The fundamental issue, given that audit commissions have been employed almost exclusively by one side of politics, is whether they perform legitimate policy and financial review functions, possibly filling in the gaps and compensating for the incapacities of existing institutions, or whether they are they primarily strategies to achieve covert political and ideological goals under the guise of contrived independent, expert advice. Walsh (1995: 328), although only commenting on commissions of the first era up until 1995, contended that while "in many respects ... (they were) driven ... by a particular political or ideological perspective and political imperatives" they nevertheless proposed overdue mainstream reforms to budgetary systems and public sector management.

2

The coming of audit commissions – pressures for their appointment

Background

Public sector 'reform' in Australia and overseas has usually been done in the past by occasional one-off, external, public inquiries that focused on sector-wide reviews. During the 1970s, a plethora of public inquiries were appointed in Australia to review state and Commonwealth public services including:

- Committee of Inquiry into the Public Service in South Australia (1973, chaired by Professor David Corbett)
- Board of Inquiry into the Victorian Public Service (1973, chaired by Sir Henry Bland)
- Royal Commission into Australian Government Administration (1974, chaired by Dr H.C. Coombs)
- Review of New South Wales Government (1977, chaired by Professor Peter Wilenski)
- Review of Tasmanian Government Administration (1979, chaired by Sir George Cartland)
- Review of Commonwealth Administration (1982, chaired by Mr J.B. Reid)
- Public Service Review Committee, Queensland (1986, chaired by Sir Ernest Savage).

Since the 1990s such external sector-wide reviews have fallen into disuse. Disillusion about the lack of implementation of their recommendations, long gestation periods for reports, and the growth of new standing administrative review mechanisms were contributing factors (Alaba 1994). Consequently, Shand (1991: 243) concluded:

> The setting up of royal commissions or committees of inquiry to look at management or administrative matters ... now seems to be regarded as a relatively ineffective way of achieving change.

Instead, public service reform became less episodic and more ongoing and unrelenting, driven increasingly by internal agencies like finance departments (Howard 1990). While, for a time, this seemed to be the pattern (Prasser and Nethercote 1993), a series of events drove the development of audit commissions as a new instrument of external review.

Factors affecting the use of commissions of audit

This background of ongoing change to the public sector, the sense that major public service reviews of the past were no longer viable, and a number of other developments in Australia at both national and state levels, triggered the development of the commission of audit as a new instrument of review.

First, from the late 1980s through to the mid-1990s there was a series of scandals about corruption, maladministration and poor economic management, and resultant budget deficits and loss of credit ratings that afflicted the long-standing state Labor administrations of New South Wales, Victoria, South Australia, and Western Australia as revealed by a series of royal commissions (Tiffen 1999). This fiscal 'crisis' prompted the need for further urgent external review by incoming non-Labor administrations. At the Commonwealth level, it was poor public expenditure control, and resultant record budget deficits at the end of 13 years of Labor governments, rather than scandals of corruption (Wanna, Kelly and Forster 2000: 224-239) that were the trigger for the first federal audit commission appointed in 1996 by the incoming Howard Government. The exception to these trends was in Queensland where, although corruption had been revealed about the 32-year-old National Party government, the state budgetary situation and credit rating had remained intact. It was institutional and electoral reform, not fiscal restitution, which was the focus of the new incoming Labor government (Hede, Prasser and Neylan 1992).

Second, oppositions that gained office during this period had mostly been out of power for long periods (see Table 1). This affected their responses to the financial crises they inherited, and their decision, beginning with the incoming Greiner Coalition Government in 1988, to adopt the audit commission model. Their long time in opposition meant that they were less trusting of the public service and existing financial agencies because of perceptions that the public service had become increasingly politicised, and, given the state of finances, incompetent too. Indeed, incoming governments saw the existing public bureaucracy as very much part of the problem. Consequently, these governments wanted their own independent sources of advice. And having been out of office for so long these new governments, for reasons of both policy and politics, were anxious to highlight quickly the flaws of their predecessors, and to be seen to be tackling the financial crises immediately. Only specially appointed audit commissions with clear terms of reference and members from outside government could achieve these goals and be seen to be directly linked to the new government's agenda.

Third, NPM with its pro-business, market-oriented, reform agenda had particular resonance with the ideological and policy preferences of these incoming non-Labor governments and was to be reflected in the audit commissions' reports.

Last, there were some historical precedents in Australia for external financial reviews. Reviews into state administrations had occurred previously (Borchardt 1970; Borchardt 1986; Zafarullah 1986). At the Commonwealth level in 1918 in the immediate aftermath of World War One, there was the *Royal Commission on Public Expenditure of the Commonwealth of Australia with a View to Effecting Economies* headed by Sir Robert Gibson which sought budget savings.

In 1973, the new Whitlam Labor Government, which had been out of office for 23 years, appointed Dr H.C. Coombs, former senior public servant and Governor of the Reserve Bank of Australia, to head the *Taskforce to Review Continuing Expenditure of the Previous Government*, which "recommended cuts in some expenditure programmes to make room for the new government's plans" (Spann 1979: 446).

More pertinent to subsequent commissions of audit were two expenditure type reviews established by the Fraser Coalition Government (1975-1983). The first of these was the *Administrative Review Committee* (ARC) under Sir Henry Bland, a former senior state and Commonwealth public servant who had also headed the aforementioned 1973 review of the Victorian public service, appointed on 22 December 1975 just nine days after the government won a landslide election victory (Wettenhall and Gourley 2009). Bland was assisted by three other members – John Reid from James Hardie Ltd, John Taylor, then a Commonwealth Public Service Board commissioner and Gerald Gleeson of the New South Wales Public Service Board. The ARC was required to identify areas to "effect economies" and to identify the means of avoiding "unnecessary duplication" (Fraser 1975). The ARC's terms of reference, mission and mode of operations were similar to subsequent commissions of audit under study here. It also invited public submissions, consulted with the states, sought the views of departments and others and produced a number of reports. These reports, classified at the time as cabinet documents, were not released until 2007. In this regard, the ARC was not different to some subsequent commissions of audit (eg Victoria in 2011). The general view is that the ARC and its recommendations were only partially accepted by the Fraser Government and was overtaken by events and the government's increasing reliance on existing agencies for advice (Wettenhall and Gourley 2009: 360). Nevertheless, given its thrust, use of external membership and methodologies employed, the ARC may be regarded as a real forerunner of subsequent commissions of audit.

The second review body of relevance to commissions of audit appointed by the Fraser Government was the 1980 *Review of Commonwealth Functions* (RCF – commonly known as the 'Razor Gang'). Established towards the end of the Fraser Government's time in office, the RCF reviewed spending and sought to consider where Commonwealth functions could be handled by the states or the private sector (RCF 1981). It was partly seen as a rerun of the ARC. The RCF was essentially a committee of cabinet chaired by Sir Phillip Lynch, a senior minister and former Treasurer in the Fraser Government, with an overt political agenda. It was criticised at the time and since in terms of its methodology, partisanship and limited policy impact (Groenewegen 1989: 252; Thompson 1989: 214-215; Wanna et al 2000: 130-132). Certainly, it was different from subsequent commissions of audit, but nevertheless provided another model for future expenditure reviews and lessons in terms of the need for a more independent format.

Numbers, appointments, features, and eras

Table 1 lists audit commissions appointed from between 1988 and 2013 (also see Appendix 1).

Importantly, all but one of the audit commissions (South Australia 2009) were appointed by non-Labor governments. Most, except for South Australia in 2009, were appointed by incoming governments generally after long periods in opposition. All commissions had relatively short deadlines – most reported within six months, with the 1992 Tasmanian *Independent Commission to Review Tasmania's Public Sector Finances* being the quickest, taking only one month, probably because its chair, Charles Curran, had chaired the earlier 1988 *New South Wales Commission of Audit*. Some later commissions took 12 months or more, and delivered several reports. These included the South Australian *Sustainable Budget Commission*, the *New South Wales Commission of Audit*, and the *Queensland Commission of Audit*. Until 2013, there had only been one Commonwealth commission, which was appointed by the incoming Howard Coalition Government in 1996. However, the new Abbott Coalition Government, elected in September 2013, implemented its election promise and appointed an audit commission in October.

Two distinct audit commission periods have been identified. The first era covered the period 1988–1996 when seven commissions were established. There was then a 12-year hiatus when no commissions were appointed, largely reflecting the dominance of Labor governments across Australia during this period. This continued until 2008 when the election of the Liberal government in Western Australia heralded the beginning of the second era. Seven commissions have been appointed between 2008 and 2013.

Table 1: Commissions of audit by jurisdiction and appointment 1988–2013

Date	Jurisdiction	Party and years in opposition	Title, chair and number of commissioners	Report date
ERA 1: 1988–1996				
1988	New South Wales	LNP 12	*New South Wales Commission of Audit* – Curran (3)	July 1988
1992	Tasmania	LP 3	*Independent Commission to Review Tasmania's Public Sector Finances* – Curran (3)	April 1992
1992	Victoria	LNP 10	*Victorian Commission of Audit* – Officer (3)	May 1993
1993	Western Australia	LNP 10	*Independent Commission to Review Public Sector Finances* – McCarrey (4)	June 1993 August 1993
1993	South Australia	LP 11	*Commission of Audit* –Thomas (4)	April 1994
1996	Queensland	NLP 7	*Queensland Commission of Audit* – Fitzgerald (4)	July 1996
1996	Commonwealth	LNP 13	*National Commission of Audit* – Officer (4)	June 1996
ERA 2: 2008–2013				
2008	Western Australia	LP 7	*Economic Audit Committee* – Marney (6)	October 2009
2009	South Australia	ALP – no change in office	*Sustainable Budget Commission* – Carmody (6)	Dec 2009 Aug 2010
2011	Victoria	LNP 11	*Independent Review of State Finances* – Vertigan (3)	April 2011 Final report not yet released

2011	New South Wales	LNP 16	*New South Wales Commission of Audit* – Stage 1 Lambert; Stage 2 Schott (9)	Jan 2012 Aug 2012
2012	Queensland	LNP 14	*Independent Commission of Audit* – Costello (3)	June 2012 April 2013
2012	Northern Territory	CLP 11	*Renewal Management Board* – Conn (4)	October 2012 (progress report)
2013	Commonwealth	LNP 6	*National Commission of Audit* – Shepherd (5)	Initial report expected end of January 2014 and final report, March 201

3

Commissions of the first era: 1988–1996

Overview

Seven commissions of audit were established between 1988 and 1996, one in each of the six states, and one by the Commonwealth. The first was New South Wales, in 1988, followed by Tasmania and Victoria in 1992, Western Australia and South Australia in 1993, and Queensland and the Commonwealth in 1996.

There were some common drivers affecting the resort to the audit commission instrument during this period. All coincided with the election of non-Labor governments after long periods in opposition. They were confronted with a public sector that had become increasingly politicised – a result of establishing a 'responsive' public service. Consequently, the incoming governments were suspicious of incumbent public servants, not only in terms of their partisanship, but also in terms of their competence. Due to the financial and budget crisis – especially in Western Australia, South Australia and Victoria following banking and corruption scandals, and to a lesser extent in Tasmania and the Commonwealth – central agencies like treasury and their personnel were seen as part of the problem. And, as mentioned, there was at this time in Anglophone countries the emergence of NPM (Torres 2004).

New South Wales

In New South Wales, the Labor Party had been in power since 1976 when the Liberal-National Party Coalition won the March 1988 election, and Nick Greiner, the Liberal leader, became premier. The extremely successful Neville Wran had been Labor premier between 1976 and 1986, followed by Barrie Unsworth from 1986 to 1988. The Unsworth premiership ended in disaster for Labor with its popularity plummeting (Cavalier 2006). The Labor government had also become associated with corruption, mismanagement, and a growing budget deficit (Laffin and Painter 1995: 1). There was a swing of more than 10 per cent against Labor, although a large number of votes went to Independents, who won seven seats (Melleuish 2006: 448).

Nick Greiner, who trained at Harvard University where he gained an MBA, was a strong proponent of NPM, and the first premier to openly and strongly embrace this approach to government in Australia. Greiner described himself as the "Managing Director of New South Wales Inc" (Hancock 2013; Laffin 1995: 76). Being out of office for 12 years, it was understandable that the new Greiner Government was distrustful of the public service it had inherited from its Labor predecessor, seeing it as partisan and biased (Laffin 1995: 74). Consequently, within a month of the election, Greiner announced the appointment of Australia's first commission of audit to prepare a state macro-financial study, and, specifically, to review public sector bodies. It had been an election promise. The chair of the Commission was Charles Curran, a businessman who was at the time Deputy Chairman of the merchant bank Kleinwort Benson Australia. The two other members were: James Yonge, Managing Director of Wardley Australia; and Jim Dominguez, Chairman of the investment bank Dominguez Barry Samuel Montagu. Don Nicholls, recently retired Deputy Secretary of the New South Wales Treasury, was also listed as a member, but was designated executive director. Laffin and Painter (1995: 9) contend that the report was largely written by Nicholls.

The Commission reported to the government in July 1988, and the report was tabled in Parliament in August 1988. The short title of the report was *Focus on Reform*, and its theme, identified on the first page as the key issue, was: "New South Wales has been living beyond its means" (Commission of Audit 1988: v). That the Commission's prescriptions reflected much of NPM ideology has been noted by commentators (Groom 1990), and was reflected in its opening statement:

> The key means of enhancing efficiency of government operations is to adopt a more commercial, market-based approach. The Commission favours an immediate move to the corporatisation of government business undertakings in order to improve returns from these operations and prepare the way for later possible privatisation of some operations. (Commission of Audit 1988: vi)

The Commission also saw itself and New South Wales as a leader:

> In the wider context, reforms in New South Wales will lead the way for other States and the Commonwealth and assist in ensuring a more secure future for Australia. (Commission of Audit 1988: viii)

The report covered NSW's financial situation, set out plans for both the long term and the short term, and discussed the financial impact of its recommendations. It also included as appendices studies of five major government business enterprises (Electricity Commission of New South Wales, State Rail Authority, Maritime Services Board, Grain Handling Authority, Urban Transit Authority), two other authorities (Sydney Opera House Trust, Sydney Cricket Ground Trust), and two community funding studies (Legal Aid Commission, Community Welfare Fund).

In addition to corporatisation and the restructuring of the public service, an important financial reform was the introduction of accrual accounting into the public sector. The Greiner Administration was the first government in Australia to do this. The 1977 Wilenski *Review of New South Wales Government Administration* had resulted in the introduction of accrual accounting in statutory authorities (Wilenski 1977). Subsequently, both the accounting profession and the New South Wales parliamentary Public Accounts Committee pressed for the introduction of accrual accounting throughout the state's public sector (Christensen 2002; Ryan 1998). Audit commissions in other states were also to recommend the introduction of accrual accounting (Ryan 1998). In addition, in other recommendations reflecting private sector management practices, the Public Service Board was abolished and power decentralised to departments. Public servants were to have greater autonomy and authority, combined with more performance monitoring and incentives, as in the private sector (Laffin 1995: 76).

This first audit commission in its thrust, processes and recommendations was to be the model for those that followed.

Tasmania

The next state to appoint a commission of audit was Tasmania, with the *Independent Commission to Review Tasmania's Public Sector Finances* (ICRTPSF) appointed by the Liberal government soon after winning the election in February 1992. Like its NSW predecessor, it had been an election promise. Since the 1989 election there had been a minority Labor government with 13 seats in the 35-member House of Assembly, supported by five Greens. The 1990s were an unsettled period in Tasmanian political life. Although minority governments have not been unusual in Tasmania, because of its proportional representation voting system in the lower house, the minority governments incorporating the Greens have been unlike earlier versions (Crowley 2003; Crowley 2008). As Crowley (2003: 61) observed:

> Green-supported minority regimes thus far have been conflictual affairs, which have not enjoyed popular legitimacy, been short-lived, and have had no effective consensus-building processes between the governing minority regime and its Green partners.

The Commission's chair was Charles Curran, who had also chaired the earlier New South Wales Commission. Other members were: John Harris, Chairman of the Trust Bank; and Bob Graham, formerly chief economist, Westpac Banking Corporation Ltd. Don Nicholls, who had been a member and executive director of the New South Wales Commission, was the executive member.

The report, *Tasmania in the Nineties,* appeared within a month, and not surprisingly, given the personnel, its recommendations were similar to the earlier New South Wales report. It discussed reducing government debt and government spending, and the need for a re-assessment of the role of government, although it recognised the particular nature of the Tasmanian economy, noting its position as an island state somewhat isolated from the rest of Australia, and traditionally dependent on the redistribution of Commonwealth funding. It also recommended that "accrual accounting should be introduced across the entire inner budget sector" (ICRTPSF 1992: 16).

There were also elements in the report that were specific to Tasmania's history and culture. For instance, industrial relations and labour market reform had not been an explicit part of the New South Wales report, but the implementation of its recommendations assumed major changes in this area. The Tasmanian report, however, was explicit about requiring that "[t]he Tasmanian labour market must be substantially deregulated" (ICRTPSF 1992: 198). Special attention was also paid to the Hydro-Electric Commission (HEC), which had traditionally dominated the public sector in Tasmania, and had pursued industrial development and quasi-political strategies beyond its technical role as a power provider. The Commission also called for a "united approach" (ICRTPSF 1992: 17). This was somewhat ill-defined, but appears to relate to the conflict between economic development and environmentalism that had been part of Tasmanian politics and society for some time. In this context the report also mentioned the possibility of cooperation between employers and trade unions "in achieving vital industry restructuring" (ICRTPSF 1992: 17).

Overall, the ICRTPSF had less impact than its New South Wales predecessor. The recommendations that were accepted included the sale of the Tasmanian Government Insurance Office and the housing loan portfolio of the Tasmanian Development Authority; small reductions in inland and payroll tax; the sale of Crown land for tourist development; and the commercialisation and corporatisation of several government agencies, including the Government Printing Office and the Forestry Commission (Dalwood 1992: 458). The proposal for a cut of 1100 public sector positions was not accepted, and the premier stated in his response to the report that the government would adopt a "gradual approach to change" (Dalwood 1992: 458). The previous Labor government had already implemented cuts in the public service.

Victoria

The next state to appoint an audit commission was Victoria, in October 1992, when the Liberal-National Party Coalition under Jeff

Kennett won a landslide election after being out of office since 1982. The Coalition came to power as a consequence of economic recession with drastic effects on Victoria's manufacturing sector, the collapse of financial institutions including the State Bank and the Tricontinental Bank fiasco, and growing budget deficits that had been subject to specific royal commissions (Tiffen 1999). Such scandals impacted severely on the Labor government's popularity and credibility with the voters (Economou, Costar and Strangio 2003: 172-175). It had attempted to refute some of the criticism of its financial management by commissioning the aforementioned Don Nicholls, to review the state's financial situation. This tactic did not work in either policy or political terms. The report, delivered to the Treasurer in September 1992, was positive about some aspects of Victoria's finances, but was generally critical of the debt position.

The Kennett Government appointed the *Victorian Commission of Audit* (VCA) a week after the election. Its appointment, once again, reflected the need for urgent action: a financial crisis, dissatisfaction with existing public service advice, support for improved managerial efficiencies, and an ideological commitment to some of the principles of NPM. It was also a clear election promise, so was not foisted on an unsuspecting public or public service. Prior to winning the election, Kennett (1992: 4) had announced in a speech on 20 September 1992, that:

> On the first day of a Coalition Government we will set up an independent audit. It will establish the true position of Victoria's assets and liabilities.

Initially, the chair was Sir Roderick Carnegie former Chairman of mining giant CRA. He resigned in December 1992 and was replaced by Bob Officer, Professor, Chair of Finance and Deputy Director of the Melbourne Business School, University of Melbourne. Other members were: David Christensen, recently retired as a Partner with Coopers & Lybrand (as it then was); and Russell Walker, as Deputy Auditor-General. The executive officer was Saul Eslake, an economist at National Mutual Funds Management.

The VCA reported within seven months, in May 1993. The first volume took what was described as a 'whole-of-government perspective' in examining Victoria's financial position, and the measures to be taken to improve it. It also examined the reasons for the state's financial position, how it compared with other states, and speculated on what would have happened if the previous government's policies had remained in place. It was, in fact, an audit of the state's budgetary situation. The second volume had more of a policy perspective and reviewed specific areas of state government, such as schools, education, public hospitals, public transport, concessions, superannuation, asset management, and government business enterprises, and it proposed a range of initiatives.

Like the 1988 NSW Commission Report, the VCA's theme was one of the state living beyond its means. It began with the statement:

> Victoria's public sector lived beyond its means to the tune of $3b in 1991-92 on a full cost basis. This loss is entirely attributable to the budget sector (departments and budget dependent statutory authorities). This represents approximately $2000 per Victorian household (VCA 1993 Vol 1: 5).

The VCA also noted that, unlike New South Wales and Tasmania, the Kennett Government was not waiting for its report to take action in relation to cutting government spending. Much of this had been done in the new government's mini-budget that was brought down within a month of gaining office (Hayward 1999: 136). Instead, the report was "much more concerned with longer-term and strategic considerations" (VCA 1993 Vol 1: 3). The Kennett Government had begun implementing policies before VCA had reported. Its emphasis was on selling government assets, corporatising, and contracting out, and it continued to do this throughout its term of office.

Unlike the New South Wales and Tasmanian governments, the Kennett Government had a more detailed plan of action before it won office, in the form of a plan for Victoria produced by the two conservative think tanks, the Institute of Public Affairs and the Tasman Institute, with the support of the Victorian Chamber of Commerce and Industry and 13 other industry associations (Cahill and Beder 2005; Hyde 2003: 328-331). The plan summarised its proposed reforms as "a major restructuring of the expenditure programs of the Government of Victoria, as well as a broad-based strategy for increasing productivity and living standards, by privatising, corporatizing and contracting out many current services of government" (Moore and Porter 1991: 1).

Like the Greiner Government in New South Wales, the Kennett Government was concerned that the public service had become both politicised, and too large. It began its restructuring by reducing the number of departments from 22 to 13, and, consequently, removing 12 department heads (Shamsullah 1993: 242). The structure has essentially remained in place under both Labor and Coalition administrations since.

Western Australia

Even before the Victorian Commission had reported, the Western Australian Premier Richard Court announced the appointment of the *Independent Commission to Review Public Sector Finances* (ICRPSF) in February 1993, three days after the election had been won by a Liberal-National Coalition. Again, it had been an election promise.

The Labor government, which had been in power since 1983, had been discredited by what became known as 'WA Inc,' a series of inappropriate relationships between government and business (Stone 1997). This led to large financial losses for the state as various commercial ventures collapsed (Moon and Sharman 2003), and culminated in the appointment in January 1991 of the *Royal Commission into Commercial Activities of Government and Other Matters*, commonly known as the WA Inc Royal Commission (Stone 1993; Tiffen 1999).

The chair of the new audit commission was Leslie E. McCarrey, the former head of State Treasury and Director-General of Economic Development. Other members were: Peter Leonhardt, Managing Partner of Coopers and Lybrand; Charles McKinnon, Managing Director of Lothbury Ltd; and Peter Unsworth, Managing Director of Unsworth Financial Services. The appointment of a former senior public servant rather than someone from the private sector as chair was a departure from the practice in the previous three commissions.

The report, *Agenda for Reform*, appeared in two volumes, the first in June 1993 and the second in August 1993. As with the three previous reports, it contained recommendations on the corporatisation, commercialisation, and privatisation of various government functions and enterprises, and also dealt specifically with "the finances and operations of major departments, government agencies, statutory authorities and others" (ICRPSF 1993: i). The report was less dramatic than those of New South Wales, Tasmania, and Victoria in that it lacked the opening statements about how the state government had lost its way that those had included.

The report did not gain the same wholehearted support as

those of the New South Wales and Victorian commissions. On the release of the second volume Premier Court created a Cabinet sub-committee to assess the report and oversee implementation, but he also "vowed that there would be no wholesale public sector sackings and expressed an understanding of the rural concerns" (Phillips and Black 1994: 249). The National Party did not support many of the recommendations, and its leader (and Deputy Premier) Hendy Cowan was concerned that there had been too much reliance on a report by the Chamber of Commerce and Industry (Phillips and Black 1994: 249). It appears that the National Party in this coalition government had more influence than it had in Victoria.

South Australia

In December 1993, soon after the release of the Western Australian report, the Liberal Party under the leadership of Dean Brown was elected in South Australia. The Liberals had won in a landslide (Marshall 1994) after a period of factional infighting within the Labor government, the economic crisis of the 1980s, and the collapse of the State Bank in 1991 that had deepened the state's already existing economic recession, and had been investigated by a royal commission (Tiffen 1999).

The appointment of the *South Australian Commission of Audit* (SACoA) was announced three days after the election. It does not appear to have been an election promise. The Commission was to report by the end of April 1994. The chair was Robert Thomas, the Chairman of Sagasco Holdings Group. The other members were: Michael Janes, the former company secretary of BHP; Professor Cliff Walsh, the Executive Director of the South Australian Centre for Economic Studies, Adelaide and Flinders Universities; and, again, Don Nicholls, as a commissioner. The report was released after five months, in May 1994.

Like its predecessors, the report reviewed the state's finances, highlighting the high level of debt and the need for a change in how services were delivered, as well as examining specific areas of the public sector. Its position was that the "public service should not have a monopoly over service delivery" (SACoA 1994: 12). Specifically, it also compared South Australia's performance to Queensland's. South Australia's credit rating had been downgraded to AA, while Queensland had retained its AAA rating.

At the end of May, the Brown Government responded quickly to the Commission's report with a Financial Statement:

> The key elements of the Brown government's proposals were: a reduction of 5,500 public sector positions over three years, including 3,000 within the next financial year, with a separation package offered to public servants providing strong inducements for voluntary retrenchment before 1 August; a two-year freeze on any budgetary provision for wage increases, meaning that any pay rise would necessitate further job losses; a cut to the education budget less immediately severe than that recommended by the Audit Commission but nonetheless aimed at saving $40 million over four years; a cut to the health budget of $65 million per annum; a plan for contracting out some public transport services by private tender; an acceptance of the Audit Commission on means testing and market-related rents for Housing Trust tenants (Parkin 1994: 398).

Queensland

Queensland was the last of the states to appoint a commission of audit in this era, in March 1996. The political situation was rather different in that its appointment followed a change of government, but not an election. A state election in July 1995 had resulted in a minority

Labor government, but after a disputed result in one electorate, and a declaration by the one existing Independent member that she would align herself with the National-Liberal Coalition, Premier Wayne Goss resigned in February 1996. As a result, the National-Liberal Coalition became the government, with Rob Borbidge as premier. Another important difference was that Queensland was not in any financial crisis, or suffering from any scandal. In fact, the Goss Labor Government had come to power in 1989 largely as a result of the findings of *Fitzgerald Commission of Inquiry into Possible Illegal Activities and Associated Police Misconduct*, which led to the end of 32 years of National Party hegemony. However, there was a perception that the Goss Government had politicised the public service and weakened the independence of key agencies, such as the Coordinator-General's Department and Treasury (Wiltshire 1992).

Again, as in the other states, the *Queensland Commission of Audit* (QCoA) was established immediately after the Borbidge Government assumed office in March 1996. There was no election promise to appoint the Commission. The chair was Dr Vincent Fitzgerald, Executive Director of the Allen Consulting Group Pty Ltd. Other members were: Jeff Carmichael, Professor of Finance at Bond University; Darryl McDonough, a Partner in Clayton Utz; and Barry Thornton, Chairman of GWA International Ltd – a clear dominance of representatives from business.

Like the other commissions the QCoA reported quickly – its report was tabled in parliament in July 1996, just four months after its appointment.

The report recognised that Queensland's financial situation was strong, and that services and infrastructure were of good quality (QCoA 1996). Pragmatically, it was thus rather more difficult for it to justify wholesale changes to the way government worked than it was in states with obvious financial problems. The Commission was obliged to argue more explicitly on an ideological commitment to competition, outsourcing, and smaller government (Ryan, Parker and Brown 2000). As one observer suggested about this part of the report, it "seemed to be based on a set of agendas currently in vogue in the Queensland Treasury" (Wanna 1997: 235).

Commonwealth

The seventh and last of the commissions of audit in this first era was the Commonwealth Government's *National Commission of Audit* (NCA), established almost immediately by the incoming Liberal-National Party Coalition government led by John Howard, which had won a landslide election in March 1996. The NCA had been an election promise. The Coalition had been out of office for 13 years – a record for non-Labor parties nationally. While the outgoing Keating Labor Government and its predecessor the Hawke Labor Government (1983-1991) had introduced many important economic reforms and adopted many ideas from NPM, this had alienated some traditional Labor voters (Keating and Holmes 1990). The Keating Government fell more from sheer policy and personnel fatigue, concern that the growing deficit indicated it had lost control of the budget and economy, and a resurgent Coalition under Howard.

The NCA chair was academic Professor Bob Officer, who had chaired the earlier Victorian Commission. Other members were: Elizabeth Alexander, a Partner in Price Waterhouse; John Fraser, Executive Chairman and CEO of SBC Brinson Ltd; and Maurice L. Newman, Chairman of Bain & Company Ltd. The executive officer was Geoff Carmody, a Director of Access Economics and a former Commonwealth Treasury officer. Access Economics had also conducted the economic analysis for the Victorian Commission (Hayward 1999: 141).

The NCA's brief was to review the state of the Commonwealth's finances, consider financial reporting processes, consider demographic issues, provide advice on setting financial performance targets, review the government's role in the economy, and improve service delivery especially in relation to the states. These were similar to state commissions. In addition, the NCA had to advise how to implement the Coalition election promise of establishing a charter of budget honesty. Additional terms of reference concerning budget honesty issues were sent to the NCA during its short lifespan.

The NCA submitted its report to the Treasurer after just three months, in June 1996. Its underlying principle was that government should confine itself to areas not able to be dealt with by the private sector, and it identified social equity and market failure as the two reasons for government involvement (NCA 1996). The NCA's report was rather different to those of the previous state commissions in its heavy concentration on government financial reporting and on Commonwealth-state relationships and related delivery issues. This is understandable given the much larger role of state governments in direct service delivery. It discussed some government services, but much less than occurred in the state reports. It proposed transferring a range of policy areas from the Commonwealth to the states, including education, health, and housing, to name just a few. Like all the previous commissions, it recommended the adoption of accrual based accounting.

Summary: processes, personnel, impacts, and lessons

Processes

In terms of processes, the commissions of audit were unlike the usual public inquiries that have been such a feature of Australian government, in terms of their transparency, level of consultation, and the perceived independence of some of their members. Nor were the commissions like a number of permanent advisory-research bodies, such as the Commonwealth's Productivity Commission, which employs an open process of investigation, releases draft reports, seeks wide-ranging inputs, and has an extensive consultation process before releasing their final reports. The Productivity Commission's reports, although economically based, are nevertheless highly regarded in terms of their methodology, and are seen as an important means of building a strong case, and, thus, support, for genuine policy change and reform (Banks 2012).

Although some commissions of audit did seek views, most information was from existing government agencies, and was more about the collection of basic required data than about promoting an exchange of ideas. Unlike public inquiries, there was, in most cases, little attempt to seek wider public submissions. Certainly, some were sought and received, but more often than not this was from groups with a predilection to support the underlying approach of the commissions, such as business groups, right-of-centre think tanks, and particular individuals. Interim reports were not used to test ideas or to seek comment for future amendment, as is the case with many public inquiries or the Productivity Commission. Certainly, as noted, some commissions released their reports sequentially in several volumes, but the recommendations contained therein were final and not for negotiation. It may be argued that the tight timeframes imposed on commissions mitigated against such consultative approaches, but many public inquiries and investigations by the Productivity Commission have similar constraints, but manage to consult effectively.

But this criticism forgets the very different purpose of commissions compared with public inquiries and bodies like the Productivity Commission. Commissions of audit were not so much for testing views and sifting the 'evidence,' and making recommendations accordingly, although they had elements of this in verifying the budgetary situation in different jurisdictions. Nor were they seeking to develop an informed consensus about what needed to be done like the Productivity Commission. Rather, commissions of audit had clear instructions about what governments wanted, and their processes and reports were to provide advice as quickly as possible about how governments would achieve this. Because many of the commissions were primarily concerned with seeking to reduce budget imbalances, they need to be assessed more in terms of managing cutbacks (Levine and Rubin 1980) than about policy renewal, although their proponents might see this assessment differently. Certainly, the Victorian audit, in its second report with its focus on a range of policy areas, was about delivering public services differently, more efficiently, and effectively. So, too, was the NCA with its discussion of transferring a number of areas from the Commonwealth to the states, seeking to go beyond the simple cut-and-burn exercise to consider how policy can be delivered more appropriately in a federal system, while based on clear principles of public policy.

Personnel

As Table 2 highlights, the commissions of this era were largely dominated by members from outside government. This allowed governments to invoke commission reports as providing independent and unbiased recommendations about what was needed to fix a failing system, but, as with public inquiries in general, this needs considerable qualification. This is because the personnel were overwhelmingly from a narrow spectrum of the business-private sector with the few academics drawn from the economics and accounting disciplines. The tight timeframes under which most commissions worked raises further doubts as to the thoroughness of their methodologies. It seemed, too much, case of appointing the members and setting the terms of reference to get the results you want – a problem commonly facing the use of public inquiries and external review bodies.

Consequently, the commissions were challenged by then Labor oppositions, and received considerable criticism from the academic community. For instance, the South Australian audit was seen by a group of academic economists as "having far reaching implications for the welfare of many thousands of South Australians" and had "exaggerated the size and scope of ... financial problems" (Broomhill et al 1994:1). Wanna et al (2000: 247) believed the NCA had negligible impact on the Howard Government. Hayward (1999), in reference to the Victorian Commission, believed it, too, had exaggerated the financial problems, was not as rigorous as it purported to be, and was concerned about the independence, bias and even, in some cases, the expertise of its members. The counter to this was the heavy support given in most cases by existing treasury and finance departments in the form of research secretariats. The NCA, for instance, had a 10-person secretariat from Commonwealth Treasury and Finance departments.

Nor should the influence of the public service, of treasuries in particular, be underestimated. Don Nicholls, as an author and member, was undoubtedly a significant figure in the New South Wales, Tasmanian, and South Australian commissions, and he also reflected the changing, and increasingly influential views, of the public sector. Although incoming governments in New South Wales and Victoria had feared a politicised public service, and set about ridding themselves of the public servants whom they saw as partisan, the treasury view had essentially moved towards a new public management one. The commissions of audit gave increased impetus to these trends.

The speed with which the reports appeared was also useful in that the voters would remember the things that they had disliked about the previous government, and be prepared to accept the radical changes being proposed not just by the commission of audit, but by the governments that had established them. Curran and Nicholls were the team that set the precedent in New South Wales; later commissions learned from what they had done.

Table 2: Membership of Audit Commissions 1988–2013

ERA 1 Membership 1988–1996								
Commission	Total m'ship	Business	Academic	Manage-ment consulting	Others	Former public servants	Current public servants	Former Min-isters
NSW, 1988	4	XXX				X		
Tas, 1992	3	XXX						
Vic, 1992	3	X	X				X	
WA, 1993	4	XX		X		X		
SA, 1993	4	XX	X			X		
Qld, 1996	4	XX	X	X				
C'wth, 1996	4	XX	X					
ERA 2 Membership 2008–13								
WA, 2008	6	X	X			X	XXX	
SA, 2009	6	X		XX	X		XX	
Vic, 2011	3			X		XX		
NSW, 2011	10	XXX	X		XX	X	XXX	
Qld, 2012	3		X			X		X
NT, 2012	4					XXX	X	
C'wth, 2013	5	X				XXX		X

Impacts

The immediate impacts of the different commissions of audit in this era were mixed. Just as audit commissions were partly a political response to certain political, as well as expenditure and administrative trends, so, too, were their recommendations to be affected by economic and political contexts.

The more dire economic situations confronting Victoria, Western Australia, and South Australia contributed to the greater enthusiasm by the governments in accepting the commissions' recommendations. In contrast, in New South Wales and Queensland the economic pressures were less, and in Queensland's case non-existent. Queensland's strong financial position – in contrast with other states, particularly Victoria – combined with the National Party's less enthusiastic embrace of economic rationalism, reduced the pressure to adopt many of the QCoA's wide-ranging proposals for purchaser–provider splits, outsourcing, tendering, and public service restructurings.

Political circumstances, where governments were in their electoral cycle, and available political capital also affected the impact of commission reports. The Borbidge Government, although new, had come to power unexpectedly and was a minority government. It hardly had time to absorb, let alone implement, the findings of the QCoA. Issues over deals with police, a flawed review of the Criminal Justice Commission, general lack of policy direction and the emergence of the One Nation Party saw the government lose office at the March 1998 elections – just 18 months after gaining office.

In other cases, the operations of non-Labor coalition politics were as much a constraint as Labor governments had had with trade unions. A strong National Party presence (as in Western Australia and Queensland), or a pivotal Independent parliamentarian, deterred an over-zealous adoption of many of the more radical commission recommendations. Coalition politics operated in Victoria, too, but the National Party held a weaker bargaining position, and, again, the perception of a dire budgetary situation set the pace of adoption.

Where the commissions of audit had a more long-term effect was in their overall contributions to further reshaping the structure and operations of the public sector. They gave further impetus to 'managerialism' and NPM, which had been driving public sector change in Australia since the 1980s. For instance, in Victoria three pieces of legislation, the *Public Sector Management Act*, the *Employee Relations Act*, and the *State Owned Enterprises Act* were passed before the end of 1992. The *Public Sector Management Act* introduced contracts for heads of departments and other senior public servants, and abolished the Public Service Board. The *Employee Relations Act* introduced individual contracts for employees in Victoria. The *State Owned Enterprises Act* was aimed at corporatising and privatising statutory state-owned enterprises (Goldfinch and Roberts 2013). Similar developments occurred in New South Wales under the first Greiner Government.

The Commonwealth NCA's recommendations built on many policies implemented by the Hawke-Keating Labor Governments, whose principles had been largely accepted. Its thrust for devolvement of key Commonwealth responsibilities – such as education and health – to the states, and other service delivery proposals, received only lukewarm response from the Howard Government, which saw it as being too politically difficult even if desired, and politically inept given the way federal-state relations are conducted in Australia. Consequently, those within government who held the relevant Treasury portfolio (Costello 2008) and external commentators (Wanna et al 2000) saw the NCA as not being a major contributor to Howard Government's long-term policy agenda.

However, the one thing that was clear about all the reports was that they appeared to advocate a revolution in how government worked. In their rhetoric about the evils of the previous government and the disastrous economic situation inherited, they were a political strategy, but they were also a comprehensive agenda for change from the non-Labor side of politics. This included the think tanks and industry associations that advised future governments, and the business community that largely supplied the chairs and members of commissions of audit.

Politically, the commissions had varying impacts. While used to condemn the previous administration for financial mismanagement, they also had adverse consequences for some of those appointing them. For instance, the Greiner Government, which first used the audit commission instrument and embraced its recommendation so enthusiastically, did suffer dramatically at the polls, partly, but not wholly, because of the 'reforms' unleashed by the Commission, and the reaction encountered from both within and outside government. After winning a landslide election in 1988, the Greiner Government became a minority government at the following 1991 election. Greiner subsequently resigned over a scandal concerning the appointment of a former minister, Terry Metherell, to a senior public service position; the Coalition government lost office in 1995 and was to remain in opposition until 2011 (Hancock 2013).

In Victoria, the Kennett Government at first weathered the initial reaction to the cuts and public service restructures well, winning the subsequent 1996 election with a large 32-seat majority. It was not until the 1999 election that the Kennett Government fell unexpectedly from office. Again, although there were a range of factors contributing to this, there is no doubt that the cost cutting, privatisation, and market orientation of the government left their scars, especially in regional areas (Costar et al 1999).

The South Australian Liberal Government, elected in 1993 on the back of the Labor government's banking scandal, was out of office by 2002. During this period it went through three premiers. Its fall from power had little to do with the SACoA report and more to do with internal frictions within the South Australian Liberal Party, mismanagement, poor leadership, and allegations of impropriety in relation to Premier Olsen.

In summary, despite the varied success of their recommendations on a macro level the commissions of audit of the first era were an early instrument in changing perceptions about how government works, especially in relation to budgetary processes and, increasingly, the delivery of services. Their hard-line, small-government agenda and support for a reconfiguration of government, although not always accepted, nevertheless helped put on the agenda the very topic of the limits and boundaries of government – areas that were to be pursued more vigorously in the second era of commissions.

4

Commissions of the second era: 2008–2013

Overview

Seven commissions of audit have been established between 2008 and 2013. The first was in Western Australia in 2008, followed by South Australia in 2009, Victoria and New South Wales in 2011, Queensland and the Northern Territory in 2012, and the Commonwealth in 2013. Of the states, only Tasmania (which has had a Labor government since 1998) did not establish one. The period of time during this second era was considerably shorter than the first. The seven commissions of the first era were established over 12 years, while the seven in the second era were established over five years. The commissions were considerably more eclectic in their membership than the earlier ones. Also, their focus was, in the main, less concerned about budgetary outcomes and more about policy delivery issues, although this varied depending on particular situations in each jurisdiction.

The first two commissions of the first era, New South Wales and Tasmania, had members consisting solely of businessmen, as did the Victorian Commission until the initial chair resigned to be replaced by a professor from the Melbourne Business School. The mixture of the academic and the business worlds was also the case for the Queensland and Commonwealth commissions, while the Western Australian and South Australian commissions each included an ex-public servant. In the second era, the inclusion of both current and ex-public servants was more common, and some included representatives from other areas. The commissions of the second era also tended to be larger. In the first era none had more than four commissioners, while in the second era two had six, and one had nine.

Western Australia

Western Australia's *Economic Audit Committee* was established in October 2008, and had been promised during the election. The election held in September 2008 produced a hung parliament, but after protracted negotiations the Liberals and Nationals formed an alliance, and the leader of the Liberal Party, Colin Barnett, became premier. The defeat of the incumbent Labor government was both unexpected and significant; until this event, Labor had been in government in all the states and in the Commonwealth (Phillips and Kerr 2009).

The chair was Timothy Marney, Director of the Department of Treasury and Finance, and the members were: Professor Peter Shergold, Chief Executive Officer of the Centre for Social Impact (a collaboration of the University of New South Wales, the University of Melbourne, Swinburne University of Technology and the University of Western Australia), and former Secretary of the Department of Prime Minister and Cabinet; John Langoulant, Chief Executive of Australian Capital Equity; Catherine Nance, Partner and Actuary, PricewaterhouseCoopers; Peter Conran, Director-General of the Department of the Premier and Cabinet; and Mal Wauchope, the current Public Sector Commissioner. This major involvement of current senior public servants as members was a departure from the previous convention of appointing members predominantly from the business sector.

The Committee's first report was endorsed by Cabinet in June 2009, and in July the Treasurer released a discussion paper that sought submissions on the Committee's five key themes. These were identified as: delivering on priorities; designing services to meet citizens' needs; maximising value through planning, competition and innovation; realising Western Australia's economic potential; and modernising public sector management. The committee also conducted a consultation based on the discussion paper.

The Committee's final report, *Putting the Public First: Partnering with the Community and Business to Deliver Outcomes,* was released in October 2009. Like previous commissions the Committee was clear that it wanted to change the role of the public sector. It argued that, "[t]he public sector will increasingly act as a facilitator of services, rather than a direct provider, with all areas of service delivery opened to competition" (Economic Audit Committee 2009: i).

The message from the Committee's report was the NPM one – of contracting out, corporatisation and the public sector behaving more like the private sector.

The discussion paper and consultation were new in terms of the way previous commissions of audit had been conducted. Equally new was the Western Australian government's establishment of an Economic Audit Implementation Team to work with the community sector. This highlighted the report's emphasis on the role of the community sector.

South Australia

In 2008, South Australia became the only Labor government to establish a commission of audit when Kevin Foley, the Treasurer and Deputy Premier, announced the establishment of the *Sustainable Budget Commission* in June 2009. Foley stated that the Commission would begin by examining the budget process and that full terms of reference would be given to the Commission immediately following the March 2010 election (Foley 2009: 3086). Fortunately for the establishment of the Commission, Labor won the election despite a swing to the Liberal Party of 8.4%.

The chair was Geoff Carmody, Director of Geoff Carmody & Associates, who had also been the co-founder of Access Economics in 1988 and the executive officer of the 1996 *National Commission of Audit*. The other members were: Monsignor David Cappo, the South Australian Commissioner for Social Inclusion in 2006; Jennifer Westacott, the National Lead Partner in charge of sustainability, climate change and water, KPMG (currently CEO of the Business Council of Australia, one of Australia's most important peak industry associations); Bruce Carter, Managing Partner of Ferrier Hodgson, Adelaide; Chris Eccles, Chief Executive of the Department of the Premier and Cabinet; and Jim Wright, Under Treasurer of South Australia. As with the Western Australian Commission, senior public servants were fully involved with the commission. More unusual was the appointment of Cappo, an advocate for social justice and social inclusion.

The first report was released in December 2009, before the terms of reference were established. The second report appeared in September 2010. The first report was a relatively innocuous document that set out principles and processes for the state budget. It was the second report, in September 2010, that followed more in the footsteps of previous audit commission reports. It listed South Australian government departments and agencies, and outlined proposed savings for each. It did not, however, contain any in-principle statements about the role of government. The events that surrounded the release of the second report might, however, have been a warning to Labor governments about taking up the political strategies of the other side. A draft version was leaked to the media before its release with warnings of a "horror budget" (Owen 2010) and, not surprisingly, it was reported that Cappo had "pleaded against" many of the recommendations (Wills 2010). The South Australian government released a response to the second report in September; it did not support many of its more controversial recommendations.

Victoria

Victoria was the next state to appoint an audit commission. A Liberal-National Coalition won the state election in November 2010, and in January 2011 the Premier Ted Baillieu announced the establishment of the *Independent Review of State Finances*. The election victory came as a surprise, apparently to the new government as well as to the electorate. Most commentators and opinion polls had anticipated that Labor would win the election (Economou 2011), but the Coalition won with a two-seat majority in the lower house. The previous Labor government had been in power since 1999. In the later years of its term in office, it had come under increasing criticism over public transport and the building of a desalination plant. The appointment of the Review does not seem to have been mentioned during the campaign.

The chair was Dr Michael Vertigan, former Secretary, Victorian Department of Treasury and Finance, and Tasmanian Departments of Treasury and Finance and Premier and Cabinet. Other members were: Professor Ian Harper, a Partner in Deloitte Access Economics who had previously been the Chairman of the Australian Fair Pay Commission and Professor at the Melbourne Business School; and Don Challen, a previous Secretary of the Tasmanian Department of Treasury and Finance. This was the first commission without members from the business sector, but its brief fell within the previous commission's tradition of reviewing government spending.

The Baillieu Government had announced that an interim report would be produced in April 2011, and a final report in February 2012. The brief (40 page) interim report was submitted to Treasurer Kim Wells in April 2011, as foreshadowed, but so far the final report has not yet been released – the only audit commission not to do so. It has been rumoured that the final report is not being released because it is too radical (Uren 2012).

Also, there has been a change of premier in Victoria, with Ted Baillieu being replaced by Denis Napthine, in March 2013. Soon after coming to power, Napthine replaced Treasurer Kim Wells with Michael O'Brien who, it was reported, "hadn't even bothered to read it" (the report) (Hayward 2013). It should also be remembered that the Victorian Government is in a somewhat precarious position in parliament. In the lower house it relies on the support of an ex-Liberal turned Independent member who is currently facing criminal charges over the alleged misuse of his government car. In these circumstances, drastic cuts in government spending and more privatisation may not be policies the government can afford to adopt.

New South Wales

The New South Wales government also appointed its *Commission of Audit* later in 2011. The election had been held on 26 March 2011, and the new Liberal Coalition government, led by Premier Barry O'Farrell, established the Commission several months later. It had been promised prior to the election, so its appointment was not a surprise. Neither was the defeat of the long-standing incumbent Labor government. A series of scandals and unpopular policies, culminating in the privatisation of electricity, had resulted in its popularity with voters falling dramatically (Clune 2011: 622). The Coalition won with a two-party preferred vote of 64.2%, a swing of 16.9%. There had also been three Labor premiers in the space of three years.

The composition of the new Commission was complex.

Stage 1 was a Financial Audit convened by Acting Treasury Secretary Michael Lambert. Stage 2 was an Expenditure and Management Audit conducted by the CEO of the Commission with an advisory board to provide guidance. The CEO was Dr Kerry Schott, a former investment banker, deputy secretary of the New South Wales Treasury and Managing Director of Sydney Water. The advisory board was chaired by David Gonski, a lawyer and businessman who was also conducting a review of school funding for the Commonwealth Labor government. There were eight other members. These were: Belinda Hutchinson, the Chair of QBE and Deputy Chair of the long established think tank the Centre for Independent Studies; Sue Page, a GP and previous National Party candidate for Richmond in the 2007 federal election; Professor Peter Shergold, who had served on the Western Australian Commission; Richard Spencer, CEO of the Benevolent Society; and Gerard Sutton, then Vice-Chancellor of the University of Wollongong. Dr Kerry Schott; Chris Eccles, Director-General of the Department of Premier and Cabinet; and Phil Gaetjens, Secretary of the Treasury were described as 'ex officio' members.

There were two reports. An interim report was presented to the government in January 2012, and released publicly in February 2012, while the final report was released in August 2012. The government issued a response to the final report in August 2012. The interim report covered public sector management, and the final report covered government expenditure. The final report built on the six themes of the interim report. The themes were devolution, partnerships and outsourcing, workforce flexibility, transparent and evidence-based decisions, collaboration and coordination, and budget constraint (NSW Commission of Audit 2012: 7-9). In its response to the final report the government gave broad support to the six themes and indicated that "[in] many areas substantial work has been commenced by the Government" (NSW Government 2012 :2).

Queensland

An election was held in Queensland in March 2012, and the new Liberal-National Party government, under Premier Campbell Newman, announced the establishment of the *Queensland Commission of Audit* five days later. It had been a LNP election promise. As with New South Wales, the defeat of the Labor government was not a surprise. The Liberal-National Party won 78 of the state's 89 seats in its unicameral legislature, with Labor retaining only seven (Williams 2012: 643-644).

However, in appointing the members, the Newman Government broke new ground for commissions of audit. The chair was Peter Costello, former Treasurer in the Howard Liberal Commonwealth Government. Other members were: Professor Sandra Harding, the Vice-Chancellor of James Cook University; and Dr Doug McTaggart, the retiring chair of the Queensland Investment Corporation and head of Treasury under the Borbidge Coalition Government. The appointment of Costello was a precedent. Although he had left parliament, it was seen as a partisan appointment and not in the tradition of appointing external experts. However, it could also be argued that appointing a former Treasurer followed naturally from the appointment of former and current senior public servants. In all three cases they would be knowledgeable and committed to a reform agenda.

An interim report was submitted to the government in June 2012, and tabled in Parliament on 11 July 2012. This dealt with the Queensland's financial position. In the introduction to the interim report the commissioners stated that two further reports would be submitted in November 2012 and February 2013. Interim recommendations were submitted to the government on 30 November 2012, and the final report on 28 February 2013. The executive summary of the final report was publicly released on 1 March 2013, and the report itself on 30 April 2013.

The interim report recommended a two-stage fiscal strategy of first achieving a surplus in 2014-15, and then a debt reduction strategy of $25-30 billion to restore the debt-to-revenue ratio to 60% by 2017-18.

In keeping with the tradition of commissions of audit, the introductory pages excoriated the previous government under the heading 'The Consequences of Ill-Discipline':

> The magnitude of the fiscal repair task is substantially larger than previously recognised, as the former Government has locked in expenditure commitments and taken unrealistically optimistic budget assumptions to mask the magnitude of the underlying structural problems (Queensland Commission of Audit 2012:10).

The report also examined the reasons for Queenslands financial position, how it compared with other states, and speculated on what would have happened if the previous government's policies had remained in place. This last approach had also been done in the Victorian Commission's report in 1992 – it appears to be a political tactic rather than a useful strategy.

The final report dealt with service delivery, government commercial enterprises, and the economy. The focuses of both the interim and the final reports were integrated by a view that the reforms to government and its service delivery were essential to the recovery of the state:

> To ensure the future sustainability of both the State's balance

sheet and operating statement in the face of a growing and ageing population, the Commission recommends the State review all current service delivery with a view to adopting higher productivity mechanisms, almost certainly with a greater reliance on private sector delivery (Queensland Commission of Audit 2013: 1-3).

The report contained sections on Queensland's economic and fiscal challenge, government commercial enterprises, financial management, front-line service delivery, and the public sector.

Northern Territory

The next commission in this era is the *Renewal Management Board* established by the government of the Northern Territory in September 2012, a week after the election that had seen the incumbent Labor government defeated by the Country Liberal Party (CLP) led by Terry Mills. Labor had been in government since 2001, but had become a minority government in 2009. The CLP won 16 seats, Labor eight, and an Independent one. The largest swing against Labor came from Aboriginal voters in remote and rural areas (Holmes 2012).

The *Renewal Management Board's* chair was Neil Conn, formerly Deputy Secretary of the New South Wales Treasury, former head of the Northern Territory Treasury and the Northern Territory Administrator in the late 1990s (the Administrator's role is similar to that of the governor in the states). The other three members were: Ken Clarke, a former head of the Northern Territory Treasury; John Gardner (former deputy head of Treasury); and Alan Tregilgas, the current head of the Northern Territory Treasury. The appointment of three former senior public servants, and the amount they were paid, were the subjects of sustained criticism from the *Northern Territory News* (Adlam 2012; Fuller 2013), which argued that the Northern Territory taxpayers were paying for advice that should have come from the Treasury. It also raised concerns that Conn, Clarke, and Gardner had also been senior public servants under previous CLP governments.

The Board released a 20-page progress report in November 2012. It dealt with the 2012-13 budget, forward estimates, the fiscal outlook and "unfunded legacy commitments" (Renewal Management Board 2012: 8-15). The previous government was, of course, the reason for all the problems identified.

A few days after the Victorian premier was replaced, the Chief Minister of the Northern Territory Terry Mills also lost office to another member of his own party, Adam Giles. Once again, a change of leader could mean a change of policy and how the Board's recommendations will be received.

Commonwealth

On 22 October 2013 the Treasurer, Joe Hockey, and the Minister of Finance, Senator Mathias Cormann, jointly announced the appointment of a *National Commission of Audit* (Hockey and Cormann 2013). The Commission is due to deliver its first report by the end of January 2014 and a second report at the end of March 2014. Clearly, the Commission's findings are expected to feed into the first Abbott Government budget in May 2014, when the final report will also be made public.

Five commissioners were appointed. The chair, Tony Shepherd, is the President of the Business Council of Australia and was the Chair of Transfield Services at the time of his appointment. He also had served in the Commonwealth Public Service, though this was prior to 1979. The other four members are: Peter Boxall, previously Secretary of the Department of Resources Energy and Tourism, the Department of Employment and Workplace Relations and the Department of Finance and Administration; Tony Cole, former Treasury Secretary and Deputy Secretary of the Department of Prime Minister and Cabinet; Robert Fisher, former Director-General of the Western Australian Departments of Industrial and Regional Development, of Trade and of Family and Children's Services, Executive Director of the Western Australian Department of State Development and the Agent-General for Western Australia in London; and Amanda Vanstone, a former senator and minister in the Howard Government between 1996 and 2007.

The composition and terms of reference of the new Commission has been generally well received by commentators (Editorial, *The Australian* 2013; Tingle 2013). The appointment of two former senior Commonwealth public servants (three if the chair is included) and a former senior state public servant, lends an air of experience, expertise and independence to the exercise. The inclusion of an eminent academic with expertise in the area, could have reinforced this further. However, there has been criticism over Vanstone's appointment. It has been compared to Peter Costello's perceived inappropriate chairing the 2012 *Queensland Commission of Audit*. Although Vanstone is not chairing the Commission, and thus less able to direct its activities, her presence could undermine the Commission's perceived independence. Moreover, Vanstone has less credibility than Costello as she had not served in any treasury or finance portfolios as minister (her portfolios were Families and Community Services, Immigration and Multicultural Affairs, Employment and Justice and Customs). Alternatively, Vanstone's inclusion has potential positives, giving the Commission an anchor in political reality and providing a link to the Abbott Government.

Another significant aspect about the Commission is its secretariat. It will be headed by Peter Crone, the Chief Economist and Director of Policy at the Business Council of Australia.

Although previous audit commissions, such as the 1992 Victorian one, have had economists from the private sector in such roles this is the first time both the chair and the head of the secretariat have come from a major business lobby group. The connection is seen to be too close by both some commentators (Grattan 2013) and the federal Opposition (Shorten 2013). After all, the Business Council of Australia is not only a major lobby group, but also in its action plan for the future of the Australian economy released in July 2013 had recommended a "comprehensive audit on the size, scope and efficiency of government spending" (Business Council of Australia 2013:46). Further, the Commission's chair, Tony Shepherd (2013), a week prior to the election wrote in the national media that a "national audit is crucial." This congruence of advocacy and active involvement in the Abbott Government's new Commission, may be seen as a potential 'conflict of interest.' We will have to wait for the final report before making any judgement on this issue.

The terms of reference for the new Commission are wide and consistent with previous Commonwealth and state commissions. First, it is required to review the "scope of government" with particular reference to federal-state and territory responsibilities and the very extent of government in relation to whether some functions should be performed at all or undertaken by the private and non-government sectors. In this the new Commission is not dissimilar to the focus of the 1996 NCA. Second, the Commission has what may be described as the usual financial/economic role to report on "efficiencies and savings to improve the effectiveness of, and value for money from, all Commonwealth expenditure" and to review the "integrity of the budget position." Not surprisingly, given this approach, the Commission's secretariat is located in the Department of Finance and will no doubt receive support from that agency.

Summary

The stated purposes of the commissions of audit in the second era were identical to those of the first era – to identify the financial wrong-doings of the previous government, to find solutions, to reduce expenditure, and to change the way governments work. But they lacked the strength of purpose and certainty. They were not composed of outsiders because, by now, senior public servants were committed to new public management and economic neo-liberalism, and could be relied on to do the job themselves. But it seemed that governments had also lost sight of the need for speed, publicity, and simplicity as a political strategy. Some reports were extremely complex, others were not released to the public, or only partially released. The appointment of a former Commonwealth minister to head the 2012 Queensland Commission was perhaps the final moment of forgetfulness about why a commission of audit needs to appear, as well as be, 'independent.' The appointment of former federal minister to the 2013 *National Commission of Audit* suggests that the appearance of independence that was a significant feature of the commissions of the first era is no longer as important. Rather, what is important is being grounded and connected to political and administrative realities.

5

Lessons for the future

In the first era, commissions of audit worked extremely well, both as political strategies and as engines of reform. They convinced the electorate of the need for change, and they were a vehicle for the introduction of the new public management ideology that, at that time, was just beginning to be accepted inside and outside of government. In the second era they had lost their way. Or perhaps they were living in the past when new public management was still uncommon. By the 2000s, NPM had become the conventional wisdom of the way government ought to work. The commissions of audit of the second era had the same ideology as those of the first era, but they were fighting a battle that had already been won.

Nonetheless, they remain a constant in Australian government and politics. In March 2012, the then Leader of the Opposition, Tony Abbott, in a speech to the Victorian Chamber of Commerce and Industry, promised a commission of audit:

> Today, I announce a further commitment to reduce the cost and complexity of government through the swift establishment of a commission of audit that will examine the detail of what the Commonwealth government does and whether it could be done better and more cost-effectively. (Abbott 2012)

Given that other audit commissions, especially the 2012 Queensland Commission, had heralded major cuts in the public sector, the appointment of such a body became an issue in the federal election campaign. There was also speculation about what it might achieve and whether it is necessary. Professor Bob Officer, the chair of both the 1992 Victorian Commission and the 1996 Commonwealth Commission, suggested that there were many recommendations from the 1996 Commission that had not been implemented and which could be revived – wishful thinking perhaps of a former commission chair! Officer's comment that politicians have political reasons for not implementing unpopular recommendations is more a truism than incisive analysis, and tells us little about the realities of political life and policy practice (Greber and Anderson 2013).

There were reasons not to appoint a new Commonwealth commission of audit. The new government has already promised to cut 12,000 public service jobs, and has abolished several agencies including the Climate Change Commission. Does it need a commission of audit, given the election promises it has already made? It can also be argued that the relatively low Australian public sector debt and deficits, and the low level of employment in the government sector, make a commission of audit unnecessary (Hayward 2013). However, this had not stopped other governments. Economic commentator Ross Gittins (2013: 30) wrote two days after the election:

> What's supposed to be next on the agenda of a new government is a first look at the books, the amazed discovery that it's all much worse than their predecessors let on, and the regretful announcement that this fiscal crisis necessitates a huge round of cost-cutting and the breaking of 'non-core' promises.

This is a perceptive summation of what many commissions of audit in recent years have appeared to be. But one of the Coalition's major planks in the recent federal election was the commitment to hold to the policies announced during the election campaign.

It will be interesting to see if the Abbott Government's new Commission learns from both the successes and failures of the 13 previous audit commissions. While no judgement of its success or failure can be made at such an early stage, and indeed concepts of success and failure are not clearly defined when it comes to commissions of audit, there are some criteria to assess its value, role and long term impact.

For instance, we can already assess whether the terms of reference are too narrow and seek to predetermine the results. On this test the Commission's terms of reference have generally been received favourably. Then there is the Commission's membership. This too has been well regarded with the exceptions noted above. Assessment of the Commission's performance in terms of its reports will have to wait. Of course, they will be evaluated by different groups from a range of perspectives – economic, political and ideological. However, even if the thrust of the Commission's proposals are disliked by some, if based on an effective consultation and information gathering process, rigorous analysis and transparent methodologies, then its legitimacy will be accepted and its impact enhanced. However, the Commission has a very tight schedule. It is expected to produce an interim report in January 2014 and its final report in March. Such urgency has plagued the quality of previous commission reports. Shepherd (2013) himself noted in his public pre-election advocacy for a commission of audit that reforms will only occur "by having a careful, respectful and honest discussion with the community about the risks and opportunities we face."

Ultimately, the real test will be how the Abbott Government will respond to the Commission's recommendations. As Abbott described the then proposed commission of audit as a "once-in-a-generation" opportunity (Abbott 2013: 3572), then his government must respond to its recommendations more assiduously than occurred with previous commissions. Failure to do so will reinforce the view that these bodies are just another prop of political fabrication further undermining the electorate's trust in government, and rendering the commission of audit instrument redundant for future use. It could also adversely affect the Abbott Government's political credibility and policy direction. The Abbott Government may surprise us in this, as it has in other areas. Certainly, there is a lot riding on the 2013 *National Commission of Audit*.

Appendix 1

Summary of commissions of audit 1998–2013

(Listed in chronological order with chair and date
of appointment in brackets)

New South Wales Commission of Audit – (Curran: 1988)

*Independent Commission to Review Tasmania's Public Sector
Finances* – (Curran: 1992)

Victorian Commission of Audit – (Officer: 1992)

Independent Commission to Review Public Sector Finances – Western
Australia (McCarrey: 1993)

South Australian Commission of Audit – (Thomas: 1993)

Queensland Commission of Audit – (Fitzgerald: 1996)

National Commission of Audit – Commonwealth (Officer: 1996)

Economic Audit Committee – Western Australia (Marney: 2008)

Sustainable Budget Commission – South Australia (Carmody 2009)

Independent Review of State Finances – Victoria (Vertigan: 2010)

Commission of Audit – New South Wales (Schott: 2011)

Queensland Commission of Audit – Queensland (Costello: 2012)

Renewal Management Board – Northern Territory (Conn: 2012)

National Commission of Audit – Commonwealth (Shepherd: 2013)

Appendix 2

Audit commission reports 1988–2012

New South Wales Commission of Audit, 1988, *Focus on Reform: Report on the State's Finances by the New South Wales Commission of Audit: Executive Summary Dated July 1988*. Sydney: NSW Government Printer

Independent Commission to Review Tasmania's Public Sector Finances, 1992, *Tasmania in the Nineties*, April 1992, Hobart

Victorian Commission of Audit, 1993, *Report of the Victorian Commission of Audit, Volume 1*, Melbourne: Victorian Commission of Audit

Independent Commission to Review Public Sector Finances, 1993, *Agenda for Reform: Volume Two*, Perth: Government Printer

South Australian Commission of Audit, 1994, *Report of the South Australian Commission of Audit: Overview*, April

National Commission of Audit, 1996, *Report to the Commonwealth Government*, Canberra: Department of Finance. Available online http://www.finance.gov.au/archive/archive-of-publications/ncoa/chap2.htm

Queensland Commission of Audit, 1996, *Report of the Queensland Commission of Audit, June 1996: Summary Volume*, Brisbane: Government Printer

Economic Audit Committee, 2009, *Putting the Public First: Partnering with the Community and Business to Deliver Outcomes: Final Report*, Perth: Government of Western Australia. Available online http://www.dpc.wa.gov.au/Publications/EconomicAuditReport/Documents/eac_final_report.pdf

Sustainable Budget Commission, 2010, *Budget Improvement Measures:*

Restoring Sustainable State Finances: Second Report by the Sustainable Budget Commission, Adelaide: Sustainable Budget Commission. Available online at http://www.treasury.sa.gov.au/budget/ initiatives-and-reforms

Independent Review of State Finances, 2011, *Interim Report*, Melbourne: Independent Review of State Finances

New South Wales Commission of Audit, 2012, *Final Report: Government Expenditure, 4 May 2012*. Available online at http://www.nsw.gov. au/sites/default/files/uploads/common/CommissionofAudit-FinalReport_RPT_v01.pdf

Queensland Commission of Audit, 2012, *Final Report February 2013*, Brisbane: Queensland Government. Available online at http:// www.commissionofaudit.qld.gov.au/reports/final-report.php

Renewal Management Board, 2012, *Progress Report 29 October 2012*. Available online at http://newsroom.nt.gov.au/rmb/RMB-Progress-Report29oct2012.pdf

References

Abbott, A., MP, 2012, *Address to the Victorian Employers Chamber of Commerce and Industry*, 9 March 2012. Available online at http://www.liberal.org.au/latest-news/2012/03/09/address-victorian-employers-chamber-commerce-and-industry-0

Abbott, A., MP, 2013, "Budget Reply," *Commonwealth Parliamentary Debates, House of Representatives*, 16 May, 3568-3575

Adlam, N., 2013, "Rent-free Living for Terry's Razor Gang," *Northern Territory News*, 22 December. Available online at http://www.ntnews.com.au/article/2012/12/22/316129_ntnews.html

Alaba, R., 1994, *Inside Bureaucratic Power: The Wilenski Review of NSW Government*, Sydney: Hale and Iremonger

Aucoin, P., 1995, *The New Public Management: Canada in Comparative Perspective*, Montreal: Institute for Research on Public Policy

Banks, G., 2012, "Independent Policy Advice and the Productivity Commission," in *Advancing the Reform Agenda: Selected Speeches*, Canberra: Productivity Commission, 121-134

Banks, G., 2013, "Public Inquiries, Public Policy and the Public Interest," *The Inaugural Peter Karmel Lecture on Public Policy*, Australian Academy of Social Sciences, July

Borchardt, D.H., 1970, *Checklist of Royal Commissions, Select Committees of Parliament and Boards of Inquiry, Vol III: Victoria, 1856-1960*, Sydney: Wentworth Books

Borchardt, D.H., 1986, *Checklist of Royal Commissions, Select Committees of Parliament and Boards of Inquiry: Commonwealth, New South Wales, Queensland, Tasmania, and South Australia, 1970-1980*, Bundoora: La Trobe University

Broomhill, R., *et al*, 1994, *Changing the Way Forward: A Critique of the Report of the South Australian Commission of Audit*, prepared by an independent grouping of academics from the University of Adelaide and University of South Australia, May

Business Council of Australia, 2013, *Action Plan for Enduring Prosperity*, Melbourne: Business Council of Australia. Available online at http://www.bca.com.au/publications/action-plan-for-enduring-prosperity-full-report)

Cahill, D., and Beder, S., 2005, "Neo-Liberal Think Tanks and Neo-Liberal Restructuring: Learning the Lessons from Project Victoria and the Privatisation of Victoria's Electricity Industry," *Social Alternatives*, 24(1), 43-48

Cavalier, R., 2006, "Barrie John Unsworth (04.07.1986-25.03.1988)," in Clune and Turner, *The Premiers of New South Wales*, 425-441

Christensen, M., 2002, "Accrual Accounting in the Public Sector: The Case of the New South Wales Government," *Accounting History*, 7(2), 93-124

Clune, D., and Turner, K., (eds), 2006, *The Premiers of New South Wales, 1856-2005, Volume 2: 1901-2005*, Sydney: Federation Press

Clune, D., 2011, "Political Chronicles: New South Wales: January to June 2011," *Australian Journal of Politics and History*, 58(4), December, 622-627

Costar, B., and Economou, N., (eds), 1999, *The Kennett Revolution: Victorian Politics in the 1990s*, Sydney: UNSW Press

Costello. P., 2008, *The Costello Memoirs*, Melbourne: Melbourne University Press

Crowley, K., 2003, "Strained Parliamentary Relations: Green-Supported Minority Government in Tasmania," *Australasian Parliamentary Review*, 17(2), 55-71

Crowley, K., 2008, "The Place of Nature? Electoral Politics and the Tasmanian Greens," *People and Place*, 16(2), 12-21

Dalwood, P., 1992, "Political Chronicle: Australia, January-June 1992: Tasmania," *Australian Journal of Politics and History*, 38(3), September, 453-460

Davis, G., and Rhodes R.A.W., 2000, "From Hierarchy to Contracts and Back Again: Reforming the Australian Public Service," in Keating, M., Wanna, J., Weller, P., (eds), *Institutions on the Edge: Capacity or Governance*, Sydney: Allen and Unwin, 74-98

Economic Audit Committee, 2009, *Putting the Public First: Partnering with the Community and Business to Deliver Outcomes: Final Report*, Perth: Government of Western Australia

Economou, N., 2011, "Political Chronicles: Victoria: July to December 2010," *Australian Journal of Politics and History*, 57(2), June, 296-303

Economou, N., Costar, B., and Strangio, P., 2003, "Victoria," in Moon, J., and Sharman, C., (eds), *Australian Politics and Government: The Commonwealth, the States and the Territories*, Melbourne: Cambridge University Press, 154-182

Editorial, 2013, "Audit commission must re-engineer out future," *The Australian*, 24 October

Foley, K.O., 2009, "Appropriation Bill," *Parliamentary Debates South Australia*, House of Assembly, 4 June, 3082-3092

Fraser, M., MP, 1975, *Media Release*, 21 December

Fuller, D., 2013, "Wrong Way, Go Back," *Northern Territory News* 7 January. Available online at http://www.ntnews.com.au/article/2013/01/07/316486_opinion.html

Galligan, B., and Roberts, W., (eds), 2007, *The Oxford Companion to Australian Politics*, Oxford: Oxford University Press

Gittins, R., 2013, "Big Change in Party, Little in Policy," *The Age*, 9 September

Goldfinch, S., and Roberts, V., 2013, "New Public Management and Public Sector Reform in Victoria and New Zealand: Policy Transfer, Elite Networks and Legislative Copying," *Australian Journal of Politics and History*, 59(1), March, 80-96

Grattan, M., 2013, "Grattan on Friday: Should a lobby group chair the Audit Commission," *The Conversation*, 25 October

Greber, J., and Anderson, F., 2013, "Abbott Told to Cut Soon and Deep," *Australian Financial Review*, 9 September

Groom, E., 1990, "The Curran Report and the Role of the State," *Australian Journal of Public Administration*, 49(2), June, 144-154.

Groenewegen, P., 1989, "Federalism," in Head, B., and Patience, A., (eds), *From Fraser to Hawke*, Melbourne: Longman Cheshire, 240-272

Hancock, I., 2013, *Nick Greiner: A Political Biography*, Ballarat: Connor Court Publishing

Hayward, D., 1999, "A Financial Revolution? The Politics of the State Budget," in Costar and Economou, *The Kennett Revolution*, 136-149

Hayward, D., 2013, "An Audit That We Don't Need," *The Conversation*, 16 September. Available online at http://theconversation.com/an-audit-that-we-dont-need-18046

Hockey, J., MP and Cormann, M., Senator, *Joint Media Conference-Commission of Audit*, 22 October

Hede, A., Prasser, S., Neylan, M., (eds), 1992, *Keeping Them Honest: Democratic Reform in Queensland*, St Lucia: University of Queensland Press

Holmes, B., 2012, *Northern Territory Election 2012*. Canberra:

Parliamentary Library. Available online http://www.aph.gov.au/About_Parliament/Parliamentary_Departments/Parliamentary_Library/pubs/BN/2012-2013/NTElections2012

Hood, C., 1990, "De Sir-Humphreyfying the Westminster Model of Bureaucracy: A New Style of Governance?" *Governance*, 3(2), 205-214

Hood, C., 1991, "A Public Management for All Seasons," *Public Administration*, 69 (Spring), 3-19

Hood, C., 1995, "The 'New Public Management' in the 1980s: Variations on a Theme," *Accounting Organizations and Society*, 20(2/3), 93-109

Howard, J., 1990, "Attacking the Budget Problem," in Kouzmin and Scott, *Dynamics in Australian Public Management*, 72-93

Howard, J., MP, 2011, (revised edition), *John Howard Lazurus Rising: A Personal and Political Autobiography*, Sydney: HarperCollins

Hyde, J., 2003, *Dry: In Defence of Economic Freedom*, Melbourne: Institute of Public Affairs. Available online at http://www.ipa.org.au/library/2002hyde_dry.pdf

Independent Commission to Review Public Sector Finances, 1993, *Agenda for Reform: Volume Two*, Perth: Government Printer

Independent Commission to Review Tasmania's Public Sector Finances. 1992, *Tasmania in the Nineties*, April 1992, Hobart: Government Printer

Keating, M., and Holmes, M., 1990, "Australia's Budgetary and Financial Management Reforms," *Governance*, 3(2), 168-185

Kennett, J., 1992, *A Fresh Start for Victoria*, Speech by Hon Jeffrey Kennett MP, Leader of the Liberal Party, La Trobe University, 20 September 1992

Kouzmin, A., and Scott, N., (eds), 1990, *Dynamics in Australian Public Management: Selected Essays*, Melbourne: Macmillan

Laffin, M., and Painter, M., (eds), 1995, *Reform and Reversal: Lessons from the Coalition Government in New South Wales 1988-1995*, Melbourne: Macmillan

Laffin, M., 1995, "The Public Service," in Laffin and Painter, *Reform and Reversal*, 73-90

Laffin, M., and Painter, M., 1995, "Introduction," in Laffin and Painter, *Reform and Reversal*, 1-21

Levine, C.H., and Rubin, I., (eds), *1980, Fiscal Stress and Public Policy*, Beverly Hills: Sage

Marshall, V., 1994, "Political Chronicle, July-December 1993: South Australia," *Australian Journal of Politics and History*, 40(2), June, 241-245

Melleuish, G., 2006, "Nicholas Frank Greiner (25.03.1988-24.06.1992)," in Clune and Turner, *The Premiers of New South Wales*, 443-462

Moon, J., and Sharman, C., 2003, "Western Australia," in, Moon and Sharman, *Australian Politics and Government*, 183-208

Moore, D., and Porter, M., 1991, *Project Victoria 1991: Victoria: An Agenda for Change*, Melbourne: Tasman Institute and the Institute of Public Affairs

National Commission of Audit, 1996, *Report to the Commonwealth Government*, Canberra: Department of Finance. Available online at http://www.finance.gov.au/archive/archive-of-publications/ncoa/chap2.htm

New South Wales Commission of Audit, 1988, *Focus on Reform: Report on the State's Finances by the New South Wales Commission of Audit:*

Executive Summary Dated July 1988, Sydney: NSW Government Printer

New South Wales Commission of Audit, 2012, *Final Report: Government Expenditure, 4 May 2012* Sydney: NSW Government Printer

NSW Government, 2012, *NSW Government Response to the Final Report of the Commission of Audit.* Available online at http://www.nsw.gov.au/sites/default/files/uploads/common/NSWGovtResponsetoFinalReport_SD_v01.pdf

O'Faircheallaigh C., Wanna J., and Weller, P., 1999, *Public Sector Management in Australia: New Challenges, New Directions*, Melbourne: Macmillan Education Australia

Owen, M., 2010, "South Australian Treasurer Kevin Foley Denies Leaking Spending Cuts Ahead of Horror Budget," *The Australian*, 15 September

Pallot, J., 2003, "A Wider Accountability? The Audit Office and New Zealand's Bureaucratic Revolution," *Critical Perspectives on Accounting*, 14, 133-155

Parkin, A., 1994, "Political Chronicle: January-June 1994: South Australia," *Australian Journal of Politics and History*, 40(3), September, 396-401

Phillips, H., and Black, D., 1994, "Political Chronicle, July-December 1993: Western Australia," *Australian Journal of Politics and History*, 40(2), June, 247-255

Phillips, H., and Kerr, E., 2009, "Western Australia: July 2008 to December 2008," *Australian Journal of Politics and History*, 55(2), June, 286-291

Power, M., 1997, *The Audit Society: Rituals of Verification*, Oxford: Oxford University Press

Prasser, S., and Nethercote, J.R., 1993, *Administrative Restructuring and Reform in Australian Government*, Canberra: Royal Institute of Public Administration Australia (ACT Division)

Public Accounts Committee, (NSW), 1996, *Pioneers – Progress but at a Price: Implementation of Accrual Accounting in the NSW Public Sector*, Sydney: Public Accounts Committee, NSW Parliament

Pusey, M., 1991, *Economic Rationalism in Canberra: A Nation-Building State Changes its Mind*, Melbourne: Cambridge University Press

Queensland Commission of Audit, 1996, *Report of the Queensland Commission of Audit, June 1996: Summary Volume*, Brisbane: Government Printer

Queensland Commission of Audit, 2012, *Interim Report June 2012*, Brisbane: Queensland Government

Queensland Commission of Audit, 2013, *Final Report February 2013, Volume 1*, Brisbane: Queensland Government

Review of Commonwealth Functions (RCF), 1981, Ministerial Statement by Prime Minister Malcolm Fraser, No 96, Canberra: Australian Government Publishing Service

Renewal Management Board, 2012, *Progress Report 29 October 2012.* Available online at http://newsroom.nt.gov.au/rmb/RMB-Progress-Report29oct2012.pdf

Ryan, N., Parker, R., and Brown, K., 2000, "Purchaser-Provider Split in a Traditional Public Service Environment: Three Case Studies of Managing Change," *Public Policy and Administration Journal*, 9(1), 206-221

Ryan, C., 1998, "The Introduction of Accrual Reporting Policy in the Australian Public Sector," *Accounting, Auditing & Accountability Journal*, 11(5), 518-539

Shand, D., 1991, "Reviewing Government Organisations: A Taxonomy," *Australian Journal of Public Administration*, 50(3), September, 242-8

Shamsullah, A., 1993, "Political Chronicle: July-December 1992: Victoria," *Australian Journal of Politics and History*, 39(2), June, 237-247

Shepherd, A., 2013, "National Audit is Crucial," *The Australian*, 30 August

Shorten, W., MP, 2013, quoted in Coorey, P., "Voters to decide on budget cuts," *Australian Financial Review*, 24 October

Singleton, G., (ed), 2000, *The Howard Government: Australian Commonwealth Administration 1996-1998*, Sydney: UNSW Press

South Australian Commission of Audit, 1994, *Report of the South Australian Commission of Audit: Overview*, April, Adelaide: Government Printer

Spann, R.N., 1979, *Government Administration in Australia*, Sydney: Allen and Unwin

Stone, B., 1993, "Accountability Reform in Australia: The WA Inc Royal Commission in Context," *Australian Quarterly*, 65(2), 17-30

Stone, B., 1997, "Taking 'WA Inc' Seriously: An Analysis of the Idea and its Application to West Australian Politics," *Australian Journal of Politics and History*, 56(1), March, 71-81

Sustainable Budget Commission, 2010, *Budget Improvement Measures: Restoring Sustainable State Finances: Second Report by the Sustainable Budget Commission*, Adelaide: Sustainable Budget Commission

Thompson, E., 1989, "The Public Service," in Head, B., and A. Patience, A., (eds), *From Fraser to Hawke*, Melbourne: Longman Cheshire, 213-239

Tiffen, R., 1999, *Scandals: Media, Politics, and Corruption in Contemporary Australia*, Sydney: UNSW Press

Tingle, L., 2013, "Good balance in this commission," *Australian Financial Review*, 23 October

Torres, L., 2004, "Trajectories in Public Administration Reforms in European Continental Countries," *Australian Journal of Public Administration*, 63(3), June, 99-112

Uren, D., 2012, "Secret Government Plan to End Big Bureaucracy," *The Australian*, 28 August

Victorian Commission of Audit, 1993, *Report of the Victorian Commission of Audit, Volume 1*, Melbourne: Victorian Commission of Audit

Wanna, J., 1997, "Political Chronicle: July-December 1996: Queensland," *Australian Journal of Politics and History*, 43(2), June, 233-239

Wanna, J., Kelly, J., and Forster, J., 2000, *Managing Public Expenditure in Australia*, Sydney: Allen and Unwin

Walsh, C., 1995, "Creating a Competitive Culture in the Public Service: The Role of Audits and Other Reviews," *Australian Journal of Public Administration*, 54(3), 325-331

Wettenhall, R., and Gourley, P., 2009, "Sir Henry Bland and the Fraser Government's Administrative Review Committee: Another Chapter in the Statutory Authority Wars?" *Australian Journal of Public Administration*, 68(3), September, 351-369

Wilenski, P., (chair), 1977, Review of New South Wales Government Administration, *Directions for Change: An Interim Report*, Sydney: NSW Government Printer

Wilenski, P., 1986, *Public Power and Public Administration*, Sydney: Hale and Iremonger

Williams, P.D., 2012, "Political Chronicles: Queensland January to June 2012," *Australian Journal of Politics and History,* 58(4), December, 638-645

Wiltshire, K., 1992, "Reform of the Bureaucracy: An Assessment," in Hede, Prasser and Neylan, *Keeping Them Honest,* 261-275

Wills, D., 2010, "David Cappo Pleaded Against Sustainable Budget Commission Recommendations," *Adelaide Now,* 16 September. Available online at http://www.adelaidenow.com.au/david-cappo-pleaded-against-sustainable-budget-commission-recommendations/story-e6frea6u-1225924930387

Zafarullah, H., 1986, *Public Service Inquiries and Administrative Reform in Australia 1895-1905,* PhD Thesis, Department of Government, University of Sydney

Zifcak, S., 1994, *New Managerialism: Administrative Reform in Whitehall and Canberra,* Buckingham: Open University Press